SOUND
AND
LIGHT

D1289539

Jack Challoner

KINGFISHER
NEW YORK

KINGFISHER
LONDON & NEW YORK

Copyright © Kingfisher 2013
Published in the United States by Kingfisher,
175 Fifth Ave., New York, NY 10010
Kingfisher is an imprint of Macmillan Children's Books, London.
All rights reserved.

Distributed in the U.S. and Canada by Macmillan, 175 Fifth Ave., New
York, NY 10010

Created for Kingfisher by The Book Makers Ltd
Illustrations: Peter Bull Art Studio

Library of Congress Cataloging-in-Publication data has been applied for.

ISBN: 978-0-7534-6974-3

Kingfisher books are available for special promotions and premiums. For
details contact: Special Markets Department, Macmillan, 175 Fifth Ave.,
New York, NY 10010.

For more information, please visit www.kingfisherbooks.com

Printed in China
9 8 7 6 5 4 3 2 1
1TR/1212/UG/WKT/140MA

Cover credits: tl Alamy/67photo; tc Shutterstock/Zametalov;
tr Alamy/Laura Johansen; bl Shutterstock/Pavel Losevsky;
br Alamy/Lourens Smak

Contents

Getting started 4

Sources of sound 6

Sources of light 8

Sound travels 10

Light travels 12

Music and tone 14

White light 16

Colored light 18

Hearing sound 20

Seeing light 22

Mirror magic 24

Bending light 26

Focus on lenses 28

Glossary 30

Websites 31

Index 32

Getting started

Sound and light allow people to enjoy and understand the world around them. But have you ever wondered what sound and light actually are? In this book you can find out. It is packed with activities you can try at home or at school that will help you understand sound and light and realize how important they are to our lives.

Warning

When you are experimenting, it is important to be safe.

Bright lights can be harmful to the eyes. Never look directly at the Sun, especially through a telescope or binoculars. If you do so, you risk being blinded for life. It is not even safe to look at the Sun when there is an eclipse.

Be careful when using electric lamps of any kind. The bulb can get very hot and cause a burn or set something touching it alight.

Sound can be harmful, too. Try to avoid very loud sounds, especially for long periods of time. Try not to listen to music too loudly through earphones or headphones, for example, because your hearing could be damaged.

See and hear

The buzzing of a bumblebee, the blast of a trumpet, the roar of a jet engine, the crack of a whip—all of these are sounds. But what is sound? How does it reach people's ears, and how do people hear?

Having problems

☹ Some of the activities in this book require patience and sometimes an extra pair of hands.

☺ If something doesn't seem to be working, read through each step of the activity again and have another try. If there is something you

A flash of lightning, the glare of the Sun, the glint of a diamond, the green glow of a traffic light—all of these are light. But what is light? How does it reach people's eyes, and how do people see?

Clock symbol

The clock symbol at the start of each experiment shows you roughly how many minutes the activity should take. All the experiments take between 5 and 30 minutes. If you use glue, allow extra time for drying.

Stuck for words?

If you come across a word you don't know, or you just want to find out a little more, look in the glossary on pages 30 and 31.

What you need

None of the activities in this book require special scientific equipment. Most of them can be done using things you can find at home, such as mirrors, batteries, and balloons.

One thing you need in many of the activities is a flashlight. Make sure that the batteries are not flat—the brighter the light, the better.

You will need eyes and ears, too. If you cannot hear or see, work with someone who can.

don't quite understand, read the explanation again or ask an adult to help you.

Try all of the activities—the more you explore what light and sound can do, the better you will understand them. Don't be scared to try your own versions of the activities as long as they are safe (ask an adult for advice). Trying something different and experimenting with new ideas are what scientists are best at!

Sources of sound

Stop and listen to the sounds around you. Close your eyes if it makes it easier. Things that produce sound are called sound sources. Most sound sources are objects moving quickly backward and forward, or "vibrating." The vibrations that produce sound are much too fast to see, but you can often feel them.

You will need:

● One piece of poster-size paper

Shock wave!

Some sounds are produced by shock waves, not vibrations. A shock wave is caused by something moving very fast, such as a bullet or a supersonic plane. You can make a loud shock wave using a homemade paper noisemaker.

A

B

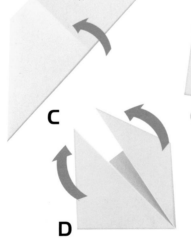

C

D

E

F

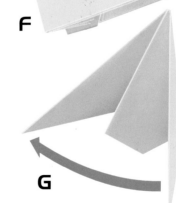

G

1 Look at the sequence of pictures (above) that show you how to make the noisemaker. You should begin by folding the paper lengthwise. The dotted line shows you where to fold.

2 The arrows indicate the direction in which the paper should be folded.

What's going on?

As the folded center of the noisemaker flies out at high speed, it pushes air in front of creating a shock wave. The shock wave is heard as a loud bang.

Make a bull-roarer

Thread one end of the string through the hole in the ruler and tie it securely. Use at least two firm knots. Go outside, away from other people, and hold the string near the free end. Now whirl the ruler around your head. You should hear a strange sound.

What's going on?

The ruler spins rapidly as you whirl it around. As it does so, it makes the air vibrate, producing the strange sound that you hear. The faster the ruler whirls, the more high-pitched the sound becomes.

3 Once you have made your noisemaker, grasp it as shown between your finger and thumb. Hold the noisemaker above your head and bring it down swiftly, as if you are hammering in a nail. As you stop, the paper fold flies out, making a loud bang.

You will need:

- A plastic or wooden ruler with a hole at one end
- A piece of string about 3 ft. (1m) long

Sources of light

Things that produce light, such as the Sun or a flashlight, are called light sources. The Sun and the flashlight bulb produce light because they are hot. This is called incandescence. Some light sources, such as fireflies and television screens, are not hot. They give out light by luminescence.

You will need:

- A 1.5-volt flashlight bulb
- A 1.5-volt battery
- A 4.5-volt battery
- A magnifying glass
- Wire with stripped ends

White-hot!

Hot objects give out red light. If they get even hotter, they give out yellow light. Really hot things glow white.

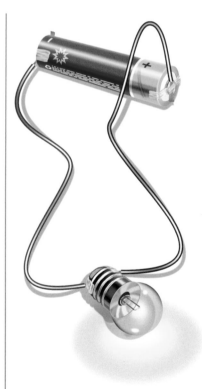

1 Look at the flashlight bulb using the magnifying glass. Can you see the filament?

2 Connect the bulb to the 1.5-volt battery, using the wires as shown.

3 Now connect the bulb to the 4.5-volt battery. What is different this time?

Sweet light

Place a few sugar cubes in the plastic bag. Find a very dark room. Stay there for at least five minutes, to make your eyes more sensitive. Now crush the sugar cubes using the rolling pin.

You will need:

● Sugar cubes
● A rolling pin
● A clear plastic bag

What's going on?

There are many types of luminescence. One of them is triboluminescence, in which some materials give out light when they break. Sugar cubes are triboluminescent. When the sugar is crushed, the atoms break apart and give out blue light.

What's going on?

The filament heats up as electricity flows through it, producing light by incandescence. With the 1.5v battery, the filament gives out yellow light. With the 4.5-volt battery, the filament is much hotter, and so it gives out bright white light.

Sound travels

The vibrations that cause sound travel in all directions as waves. If you shouted to someone standing 1,116 ft. (340m) away from you, the sound of your voice would take about one second to reach the other person. Most of the sound we hear travels through the air, but sound can also travel through solids and liquids.

You will need:

- A pitcher
- Water
- A shallow tray
- Two pencils

Air waves

Sound waves spread out in all directions, just like water waves. This is why a sound becomes quieter the farther you are from it. A megaphone prevents sound from becoming too spread out.

1 Put some water from the pitcher into the tray. Wait for it to settle.

2 Touch your finger on the water's surface. Move your finger up and down to produce water waves that travel in every direction, just like sound waves through the air.

3 Place the pencils into the water, as shown above. Make waves again where the pencils are close together. What happens to the waves now?

String sounds

Tie about 16 in. (40cm) of string or thread to the spoon, near the middle. Wrap the free end of the string around your finger and swing the spoon so that it knocks against the table. Now do the same again, but this time quickly put the finger with the string wrapped around it next to your ear.

You will need:

● String or thread
● A large spoon
● A table or chair

What's going on?

Sound travels through solids faster, and often more clearly, than through the air. The spoon makes a sound as it vibrates after hitting the table. The sound waves spread out in air, so it sounds quiet. Sound waves in the string do not spread out as they travel up the string.

What's going on?

The more spread out a sound wave is, the quieter the sound. The pencils in the water do not allow the water waves to spread out so much. In the same way, the sides of a megaphone do not allow the sound waves to become so spread out, either.

11

Light travels

When you turn on a flashlight, the bulb seems to light up immediately. Actually, it takes a short time for the light in the flashlight to travel to your eyes—less than a hundred-millionth of a second! Even though it travels at such an incredible speed, light from the Sun takes eight minutes to reach us on Earth. Light does not travel through all materials, though. Where an object stops the passage of light, a shadow may form.

What's going on?

When light from the flashlight hits the particles of talcum powder bounces off in all directions. Some of light makes it into your eyes, so you see the path of the beam. When the a clear, and there is nothing to bounce t light into your eyes, the beam of light goes past you without you seeing it.

Seeing the light

You can only see light when it shines into your eyes! To do all these steps together, try this experiment when it is dark outside.

You will need:

- A flashlight
- Some newspaper
- Talcum powder
- A friend

1 Put some newspaper down in a room to protect the floor and make the room dark.

2 Ask a friend to shine the flashlight from one side of the room to the other, so that the light beam passes in front of your eyes. You cannot see the beam.

3 Sprinkle the talcum powder in the path of the light beam. Suddenly you can see where the light is going. What happens if your friend blocks part of the beam with a finger?

Passing through

Ask a friend to shine a flashlight in your direction, but not directly into your eyes. What happens if he or she holds different materials in front of the flashlight? Try clear plastic, tracing paper, wood, metal, and your hand.

You will need:

- A flashlight
- Objects made of different materials

4 Take the flashlight outside when it is dark. Shine it straight up into the air. Only if it is misty or foggy will you be able to see the light beam.

Music and tone

Sound is caused by vibration. All sound is high or low depending on how fast the vibrations are that cause it. Music is sound that has a beautiful or interesting mixture of different vibrations. There are three types of musical instruments: percussion, such as drums, which resound when hit; wind instruments, such as clarinets, where the air inside vibrates; and string instruments, such as violins and guitars, that sound when plucked or bowed.

You will need:
- An empty shoebox
- Large rubber bands
- Scissors
- Glue
- Two pieces of wood about 1/3 in. (1cm) thick and as wide as the shoebox

Rubber-band guitar
Make your own guitar using rubber bands, some wood, and a shoebox.

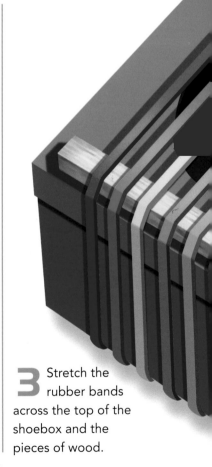

1 Remove the lid from the shoebox and cut a hole in the top.

2 Using the glue, stick one piece of wood to each end of your shoebox on either side of the hole you have cut out. Leave to dry.

3 Stretch the rubber bands across the top of the shoebox and the pieces of wood.

What's going on?

When you pluck the rubber bands, they vibrate and make a sound. The entire box vibrates, which makes the sound louder. You can raise the pitch of the note in three ways: a rubber band will produce a higher note the more it is stretched, the shorter it is, and the thinner it is.

Leave a gap of about 1/3 in. (1cm) between each rubber band. Press one finger on the rubber bands at different distances while you pluck with your other hand to play different notes.

Low and high

Low-pitched sounds are produced by slow vibrations, and high-pitched sounds are produced by more rapid vibrations. Listen carefully for the different high-and low-pitched sounds caused by the amount of water in the bottle and by how strongly you blow across it.

You will need:

- A plastic bottle
- A pitcher of water

What's going on?

The column of air inside the bottle vibrates when you blow across the top of the bottle. The shorter the air column, the faster the air vibrates, and so the higher the note is.

White light

Most light sources, including the Sun and flashlights, give out "white light." It is given this name because it seems to have no color. In fact, white light has more color than any other type of light. White light is a mixture of many colors, from red to violet. In some situations, all the colors separate out to produce a continuous band of color called the white light spectrum. For example, a rainbow forms when raindrops separate sunlight into a spectrum.

You will need:
- A CD
- A flashlight
- Aluminum foil

Compact spectrum

You can produce a spectrum with a compact disk (CD). Take care not to touch or scratch the CD's shiny surface when handling it.

1 Make a hole about ⅕ in. (0.5cm) in diameter in the middle of the foil. Wrap the foil over the front of the flashlight. Make sure the hole is in the middle.

2 Place the CD on a table, with the shiny side facing upward.

3 Turn on the flashlight and hold it so that light reflects off the CD and into your eyes. Keep the CD between you and the flashlight.

What's going on?

The surface of a CD is covered with very small dents, called pits. These cause each color of light to reflect at a slightly different angle, producing the spectrum.

Homemade rainbow

Fill the plant sprayer with water and set the spray to produce a fine mist. Stand with your back to the Sun. Try to face something dark, such as a large bush. This experiment works best in the morning or the evening, when the Sun is not very high in the sky. Spray water in front of you. You will see a band of colors from red to violet (the spectrum)—your very own rainbow!

You will need:

- A water mister for spraying plants
- A sunny day

What's going on?

You should be able to see the seven main color regions in the spectrum: red, orange, yellow, green, blue, indigo, and violet.

Point the flashlight diagonally downward, as shown above.

Colored light

A theater stage can be lit up with colored lights by shining a white spotlight through a colored filter. The brake lights at the back of a car look red because they shine through a red plastic filter. Filters remove certain colors from white light, but allow the rest of the spectrum through. Some light sources produce only certain colors of the spectrum.

You will need:
- A glass bowl filled with water
- A flashlight
- Milk
- A teaspoon

Why is a sunset orange?

As the Sun's white light passes through the air, only the red, orange, and yellow light gets through—the blue and greens are scattered.

1 Shine the flashlight toward you, straight through the bowl of water. What color is the light?

2 Add about half a teaspoon of milk to the water and stir it in thoroughly.

3 Again, shine the flashlight through the water. What color is the light now?

18

What's going on?

Tiny particles of fat in the milk scatter blue and green light more than they scatter other colors. The same thing happens to the blue and green parts of sunlight as it passes through the air.

Lose the blues

Make a spectrum using a CD (see page 16). Hold the yellow folder between the flashlight and the CD. This makes the light beam yellow. Is the spectrum the same?

You will need:

- A clear yellow plastic folder
- A flashlight
- Aluminum foil
- A CD

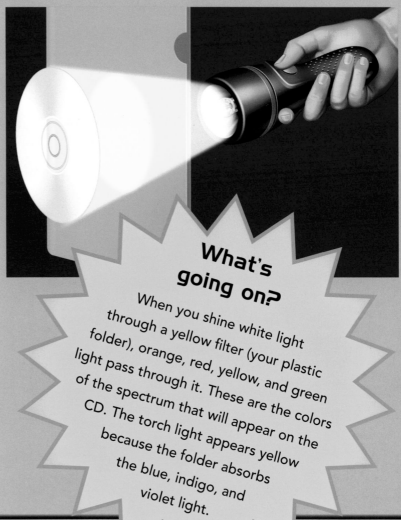

What's going on?

When you shine white light through a yellow filter (your plastic folder), orange, red, yellow, and green light pass through it. These are the colors of the spectrum that will appear on the CD. The torch light appears yellow because the folder absorbs the blue, indigo, and violet light.

Hearing sound

When sound waves enter your ear, a tiny membrane of skin vibrates. These vibrations pass deep into the ear, where they are detected by nerves that send messages to the brain. Sources of sound that are very loud or close make the membrane vibrate more than those that are quiet or far away. Very loud sounds can damage your ears.

You will need:

● A balloon
● Sugar (granulated)
● A glass or plastic cup
● Scissors
● Rubber band

What's in an ear?

When the eardrum moves back and forth, it vibrates three tiny bones (the smallest in your body). The last bone vibrates a membrane in an organ called the cochlea. The cochlea is filled with fluid and is lined with tiny hairs. The vibrations pass through the fluid and vibrate the hairs. The hairs are attached to nerves that pass on the information about the vibrations to your brain.

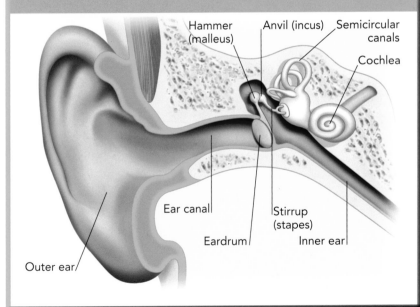

Hammer (malleus) Anvil (incus) Semicircular canals

Cochlea

Ear canal

Stirrup (stapes)

Eardrum

Inner ear

Outer ear

Ear drum

Sound makes a stretched rubber band vibrate, in exactly the way it causes your eardrum to vibrate.

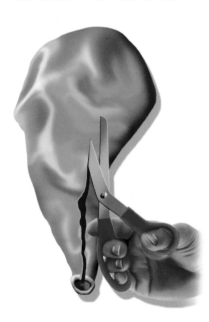

| Cut the balloon and open it out to form a sheet of rubber large enough to fit over the top of the cup.

What's going on?

The sound waves hitting the rubber sheet cause it to vibrate. This is exactly what happens when sound hits your eardrum. You can see this because the sugar grains dance up and down. When your ears are covered, some of the sound waves are absorbed and the noise does not sound so loud.

2 Stretch the rubber sheet over the top of the cup and attach it to the cup using the rubber band so that the sheet stays taut.

3 Sprinkle a few sugar grains onto the rubber sheet. Now shout, play music, or make another loud noise close to the rubber sheet. What happens to the sugar?

Seeing light

Light from light sources, or light that has reflected off other objects, enters our eyes through a lens (see pages 28–29). The lens forms a picture, called an image, at the back of the eye. The back of the eye is connected to the brain by a bundle of nerves. Our eyes hold an image of what we see for about a quarter of a second after the light has entered our eyes.

What's going on?

You should see an image of the arrow at the back of the balloon. The image is upside down, or inverted, because the magnifying glass makes the light rays cross over each other as they pass through the balloon. Images in the eye are inverted, too, but the brain interprets them so we see them the right way up.

You will need:

- A balloon
- A square of cardboard
- Scissors
- A flashlight
- A magnifying glass
- Tape

Model of the eye

To see how the eye forms an image, make a simple model using a balloon.

I   Fill the balloon with water until the balloon is about 4 in. (10cm) in diameter. Tie the balloon firmly, so that the water cannot escape.

2   Cut a piece of cardboard to fit over the front of the flashlight. Cut an arrow-shaped slit in the cardboard, as shown, and stick it to the flashlight.

3   Hold the magnifying glass right in front of the balloon. Now point the flashlight at the balloon and turn it on.

Fooling the eye

In a dark room, turn on the lamp and hold the CD underneath the bulb. Look closely at the spectrum this produces. Is it a complete spectrum? Which colors are missing?

You will need:

- A CD
- A lamp with an energy-saving bulb

What's going on?

Fluorescent lamps, such as energy-saving light bulbs, appear white. But they do not produce all the colors of the spectrum, like the Sun or an incandescent lamp, does. They fool the eye into seeing white by producing red, green, and blue light.

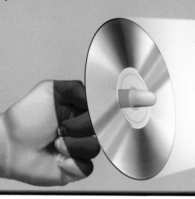

Mirror magic

Have you ever seen your reflection in a store window? Any shiny surface can act as a mirror, but the mirrors in your home reflect all the light that falls on them. The picture, or image, in a mirror is reversed—right becomes left, and left becomes right. Curved mirrors can make things become reversed, too, and they can make things look bigger, smaller, or even upside down.

What's going on?

Most of the light that hits a clear plastic or glass surface passes through—this is why you can see you friend in step 3. Some light reflects of the plastic surface, and when there is n light passing through from the other side, you can see the reflected light. This is why you see yourself in step 2.

Seeing it both ways

A piece of clear plastic can act as a mirror on both sides.

1 In a dark room, face your friend and stand about 3 ft. (1m) away. Hold the plastic vertically, halfway between you.

2 Shine the flashlight at your face. You should see your reflection in the plastic. What does your friend see?

3 Ask your friend to shine the flashlight on his or her face. Now you should be able to see your friend's face clearly.

You will need:

- A flat sheet of clear plastic from a picture frame
- A flashlight
- A friend

Magic window picture

Face a window and hold the paper in front of your face. Now hold the mirror so that it faces away from you and light from the window reflects onto the paper. Make the distance between the mirror and the paper about 6 in. (15cm). The window's image should appear on the paper. Alter the distance between the mirror and the paper if you do not see the image right away.

You will need:

- A magnifying makeup or shaving mirror
- White paper

This is because the light has bounced off it and passed through the plastic. What does your friend see now?

What's going on?

Because the mirror curves inward, light is brought together, or focused. This is how it is possible to produce a bright image on the paper.

Bending light

In a swimming pool, you may have noticed that people swimming underwater look different from how they look out of the water. Light that has reflected off their bodies bends as it leaves the water. This bending of light is called refraction, and it happens whenever light passes from one transparent substance to another.

What's going on?

The milk in the water allows you to see the path of the light more clearly. You will see the light bend as it enters the bowl. The beam of light changes direction slightly as it moves from air, through the glass, and into the milky water. This is known as refraction.

Watch it bend

In this experiment, you can watch a beam of light bending as it enters a bowl of water.

You will need:

- A flashlight
- Cardboard, tape, and scissors
- A glass bowl filled with water
- Milk

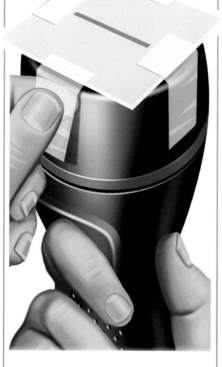

1 Cut a piece of cardboard to cover the front of the flashlight. Make a slit in the middle, about 1/5 in. (0.5cm) wide. Tape the piece of cardboard over the flashlight.

2 Add a few drops of milk to the water and mix it in well.

More or less

Find somewhere lit up by bright sunlight. On a dull day, use the flashlight. Fill the dish with water and place it where light shines into it. Stand the mirror against one end of the dish, sloping as shown. Hold the paper vertically in front of the dish, so that light reflecting off the mirror hits it. You may also see a patch of light on the wall.

You will need:

- A sunny day or a flashlight
- A flat mirror
- A shallow dish
- Water
- White paper

What's going on?

Sunlight (or light from the flashlight) is a mixture of many colors. Each light color refracts at a slightly different angle, so the colors spread out and form a bright section of colors, which are reflected onto the paper.

3 Make the room dark and shine the flashlight into the bowl at an angle. Vary the angle and watch the path of light inside the milky water.

Focus on lenses

Cameras, binoculars, slide projectors, and microscopes all use lenses—specially shaped pieces of transparent material (usually glass) that can make things look bigger, smaller, nearer, or farther away than they really are, or even upside down. And all because light refracts as it passes through the lens. We all have lenses in our eyes. Sometimes these lenses are faulty—that's when we need to wear glasses or contact lenses.

Slide projector

A lens can project an image onto a wall. You can even use a lens to make a simple slide projector, making a shape appear much bigger than it really is.

You will need:

- A magnifying glass
- A desk lamp
- A piece of paper with a shape cut out of it

▌Make the room dark. Turn on the lamp and hold the paper in front of it. Do not hold it too close, as the lamp could be hot.

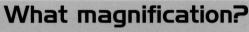

What's going on?

Light from the lamp passes through the paper and then refracts as it passes through the magnifying glass. An image of the shape will only form on the wall or ceiling if the magnifying glass is at just the right distance from the paper.

What magnification?

Draw a line 1 in. (2.5cm) long on the paper. Look at the line through the magnifying glass and draw how big the line looks. Measure the line you have drawn.

You will need:

- A magnifying glass
- Paper
- A pencil
- A ruler

2 Hold the magnifying glass about 4 in. (10cm) above, or in front of, the paper. You should see an image of the cut-out shape on the ceiling or wall.

What's going on?

A magnifying glass is a type of lens used to look at very small things. The length (in inches) of the new line you have drawn is the magnification of the magnifying glass. For example, if you drew a line that is 2½ in. (6cm) long, your magnifying glass has a magnification of 2.5x.

Glossary

COCHLEA A spiral-shaped part of the inner ear that contains fluid and many thousands of hairs. The fluid and hairs vibrate when sound travels through them and then nerves pick up this information and pass it on to the brain. The brain then interprets the signals that it receives as sound.

CONCAVE MIRROR A mirror with a reflective surface that curves inward.

EARDRUM A tiny membrane of skin inside the ear that vibrates when sound waves enter the ear. The vibrations are passed deeper into the ear and are detected by nerves that send messages to the brain, where they are interpreted as sound.

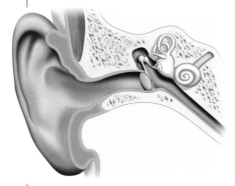

EAR PROTECTORS
Protective coverings for the ears that people wear in noisy places such as factories to prevent damage to their hearing. Most ear protectors are made of material containing a lot of air holes, which help absorb loud noises.

FILAMENT A thin metal wire in a light bulb. The filament heats up to high temperatures when electricity passes through it. This causes it to produce light through incandescence.

FILTER A clear screen, through which light can pass, that removes certain colors from white light and allows the rest of the spectrum through.

FLUORESCENT Light given out by some materials when they absorb various kinds of energy. The inside of a fluorescent lamp is coated with a material that absorbs ultraviolet light and changes it into visible light.

FOCUS A way of bringing something together and concentrating it in one place, as when light is focused in a concave mirror.

FREQUENCY How often something happens. For example, a source of sound that vibrates many times a second has a high frequency.

IMAGE A picture or likeness of a person or thing produced from a mirror, through a lens, or by electrical means on a screen.

INCANDESCENCE Light given out from objects, such as the Sun, because they are hot. An incandescent lamp produces light because its electrical filament becomes hot.

LENS Specially shaped pieces of transparent material that can make things look bigger, smaller, nearer, or farther away. They do this by bending light as it passes into them and then out again.

LUMINESCENCE
Light given out from objects, such as fireflies and television screens, produced by methods other than heating.

MEMBRANE A thin, flexible piece of skin that connects or covers parts of a living thing or separates one part of a living thing from another.

NERVE A pathway that carries messages between the brain and other parts of the body.

PITCH The way something sounds high or low, such as the different notes in a musical scale.

PRISM A transparent block of glass or plastic with several sides, which can separate light passing through it into the colors of the spectrum.

REFLECTION The bouncing back of light or sound from a surface—for example, light from a mirror or sound from the walls on the inside of a tunnel.

REFRACTION The way light bends as it passes from one different substance to another—for example, from air to water, or from air to glass.

SHOCK WAVE A disturbance in the air that travels out in all directions. It is a sound wave that is heard as a loud sound when it reaches your ears. For example, the sound of thunder is produced by a shock wave.

SOURCE The place from which sound or light comes. For example, the Sun is a source of light, and a CD player is a source of sound. The energy of both sound and light travels by means of waves.

SPECTRUM   A band of colors that together make up white light, but that can sometimes be separated out—for example, by raindrops or a prism—into the seven color regions seen in rainbows: (red, orange, yellow, green, blue, indigo, and violet).

TRANSLUCENT   A material is translucent if it lets some light through, but not enough to see through it completely.

TRANSPARENT   A material is transparent if it lets nearly all the light through so you can see through it clearly—for example, glass.

TRIBOLUMINESCENCE   When something gives out light if it is rubbed, scratched, or broken.

VIBRATION   Something moving very quickly backward and forward. Sound is produced because of vibrations in the air. Sometimes, vibrations can be felt as well as heard.

VOCAL CORDS   A pair of membranes found in the larynx, or voice box. When we breathe air into them from the lungs, they vibrate and produce the sound of our voice. This sound varies in pitch, depending on whether the cords vibrate quickly (high sounds) or slowly (low sounds).

WAVE   A disturbance of the air. Waves travel from a source of sound in all directions. When they reach your ears, you hear a sound. It is useful to picture sound waves traveling through the air like ripples in a pond.

Websites

If you have enjoyed this book, the websites below will give you even more information on sound and light. Many of them have fun games to play that will help you understand the difficult sections.

Sound:
- http://science.education.nih.gov/supplements/nih3/hearing/activities/lesson3.htm
- www.fossweb.com/modules3-6/PhysicsofSound/index.html
- www.engineeringinteract.org/resources/oceanodyssey/flash/concepts/sourcesofsound.htm

Light:
- www.bbc.co.uk/schools/ks2bitesize/science/physical_processes/light_shadows/read1.shtml
- www.nationalmediamuseum.org.uk/nmem/magic-factory/index2.html
- www.engineeringinteract.org/resources/alienattack/alienattacklink.htm
- www2.bgfl.org/bgfl2/custom/resources_ftp/client_ftp/ks1/science/colour_and_light/index.cfm

Index

OCT __ 2013

A B C
airplanes, supersonic 6
beams, light 12, 13, 26

D E
ears 20
eyes 22–23

F
filaments 8
filters 18

G H
hearing 20–21

I J K
images 22, 24, 25, 28, 29
incandescence 8
instruments, musical 14–15

L
lenses 22, 28–29
light
  beams of 12, 13, 26
  bending 26

colored 9, 18–19, 23, 27
colors of 8, 16–17
filters 18–19
fluorescent 23
focusing 25
reflecting 24–25
sources of 8, 16, 18
traveling 12, 18-19, 26–27
luminescence 8

M
magnification 29
materials
  translucent 13
  transparent 13
mirrors 24–25
music 14–15

N O
notes, musical 14–15
objects, opaque 13

P
pitch 14–15

Q R
rainbows 17
refraction 26–27, 28

S
shadows 12
shock waves 6
sight 22–23

T
triboluminescence 9

V
vibrations 6, 14

W X Y Z
white light 9, 16
white light spectrum 16